NIGHTMARE PLAGUES

TUBERCULOSIS
The White Plague!

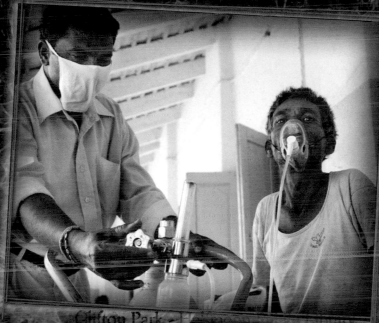

by Miriam Aronin

Consultant: Irina Gelmanova, MD, MPH

BEARPORT
PUBLISHING

New York, New York

Credits

Cover and Title Page, © Noah Seelam/AFP/Newscom; 4, AP Images/Lynne Sladky; 5, Noah Seelam/AFP/Newscom; 6T, AP Images/Lynne Sladky; 6B, Sukree Sukplang/Reuters/Landov; 7T, © Clark Overton/Phototake, Inc; 7B, © Nancy Kaszerman/ZUMA Press/Newscom; 8L, © SPL/Photo Researchers, Inc.; 8R, Courtesy of Sarah Mitchell/ University of York; 9, © AKG Images/British Library; 10L, © The Granger Collection, New York; 10R, © The Granger Collection, New York; 11, Everett Collection/SuperStock; 12L, © Stefano Bianchetti/Corbis; 12R, © Eye of Science/ Photo Researchers, Inc.; 13, © Lester V. Bergman/Corbis; 14, Courtesy of the Adirondack Collection, Saranac Lake Free Library, #95.202; 15, Courtesy of the Adirondack Collection, Saranac Lake Free Library, #P82.26; 16, Courtesy of Mwanner; 17T, Courtesy of the Adirondack Collection, Saranac Lake Free Library, #P84.25; 17B, Courtesy of the Adirondack Collection, Saranac Lake Free Library, #87.674d; 18L, © The National Library of Medicine, Bethesda, Maryland; 18R, © The National Library of Medicine, Bethesda, Maryland; 19, Courtesy of Rocky Mountain Laboratories/NIAID/NIH/Hamilton, Montana; 20, © Tang Chhin Sothy/AFP/Newscom; 22, © Denis Meyer/Imagebroker/Alamy; 23, © AP Images/Themba Hadebe; 24, © Fred R. Conrad/The New York Times/Redux; 25, © Damon Higgins/The Palm Beach Post/ZUMA Press/Newscom; 26, © Damon Higgins/The Palm Beach Post/ ZUMA Press/Newscom; 27, © Indranil Mukherjee/AFP/Getty Images; 28, © Abdullah Freres/Corbis; 29, © Francisco Matarazzo Sobrinho Collection, Sao Paulo/SuperStock.

Publisher: Kenn Goin
Senior Editor: Lisa Wiseman
Creative Director: Spencer Brinker
Design: Dawn Beard Creative
Photo Researcher: Jennifer Bright

Library of Congress Cataloging-in-Publication Data

Aronin, Miriam.
   Tuberculosis : the white plague! / by Miriam Aronin.
      p. cm. — (Nightmare plagues)
   Includes bibliographical references and index.
   ISBN-13: 978-1-936088-06-5 (library binding)
   ISBN-10: 1-936088-06-1 (library binding)
   1. Tuberculosis. I. Title.
   RA644.T7A76 2011
   616.9'95—dc22   8.214
                                    2010010679

For more information, write to Bearport Publishing Company, Inc., 101 Fifth Avenue, Suite 6R, New York, New York 10003. Printed in the United States of America in North Mankato, Minnesota.

072010
042110CGF

10 9 8 7 6 5 4 3 2 1

Contents

Something Really Bad

In the fall of 2007, Oswaldo Juarez (oz-WAWL-doh HWAHR-ez), a 19-year-old student in Florida, fell ill. For more than two weeks, he suffered from a hacking cough and high fevers.

Then one night, Oswaldo felt so bad that he thought he might be dying. His chest ached. He had so much trouble breathing that he couldn't sleep. Around 4:00 A.M., he ran to his bathroom. There, he coughed up blood into the sink. That was the moment he knew he had "something really bad," he said.

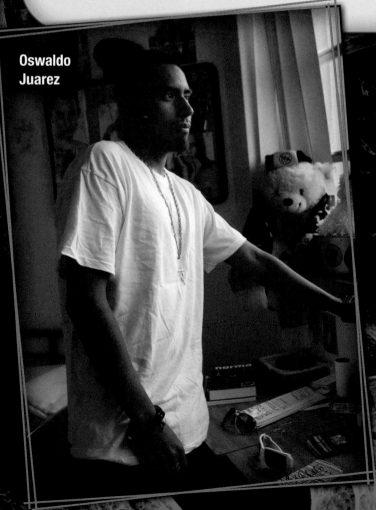

Oswaldo Juarez

Oswaldo came to the United States from Peru, a country in South America, to study English.

Oswaldo rushed to see a doctor. The doctor did tests and gave him the terrible news. Oswaldo had **pulmonary tuberculosis**, or TB—a disease that attacks a person's lungs and can be deadly if not treated. Doctors believe Oswaldo caught TB in his home country before he left for Florida.

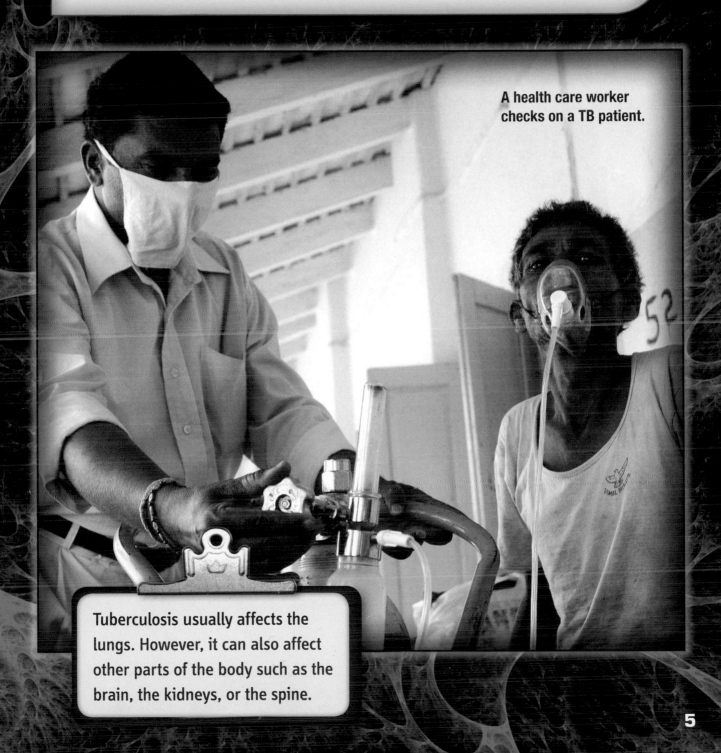

A health care worker checks on a TB patient.

Tuberculosis usually affects the lungs. However, it can also affect other parts of the body such as the brain, the kidneys, or the spine.

A Giant Hole

Doctors took **X-rays** and found that tuberculosis had torn into Oswaldo's right lung. There was a large hole, about the size of a golf ball, where lung **tissue** used to be. This kind of lung damage brings on horrible symptoms. For example, TB patients have trouble breathing. They often have long-lasting coughs, fever, chills, weight loss, and chest pain.

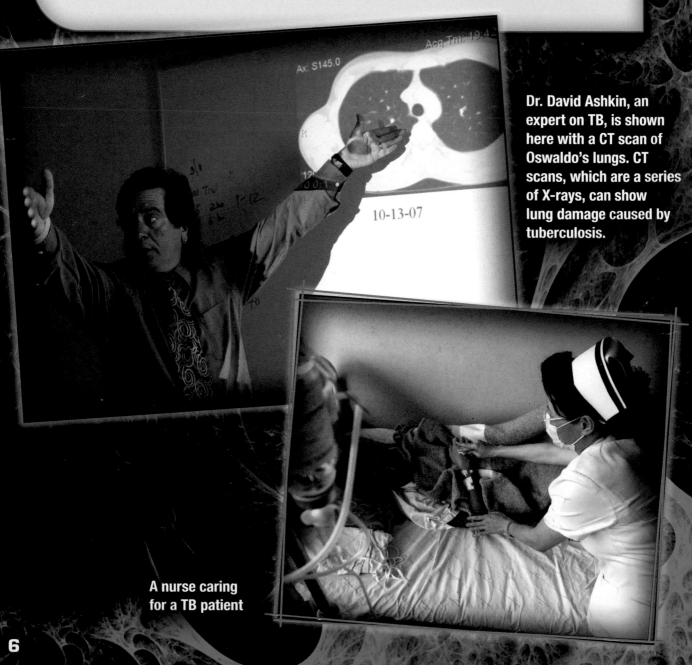

Dr. David Ashkin, an expert on TB, is shown here with a CT scan of Oswaldo's lungs. CT scans, which are a series of X-rays, can show lung damage caused by tuberculosis.

A nurse caring for a TB patient

Without treatment, tuberculosis attacks more and more of a patient's lung tissue. Eventually, he or she can no longer breathe and will die. To save his lungs and his life, doctors gave Oswaldo medicines called **antibiotics**. Unfortunately, none of the medicines his doctors tried at first worked.

Healthy lungs

When a TB patient's lungs become damaged, **blood vessels** in the lungs can break open. Then the patient may start coughing up blood, just like Oswaldo did.

These lungs were infected with TB. It can take months or even years for the disease to cause a hole, such as the one in Oswaldo's lung, to develop. Many people who have TB don't always feel sick at first, so they don't know that they have the disease until it's so far advanced that it has caused harm to their bodies.

A Mysterious Disease

Oswaldo's doctors knew how deadly tuberculosis could be. The disease has been killing people for more than 4,000 years. Around 2,500 years ago, the famous Greek doctor Hippocrates (hih-PAH-kruh-teez) identified tuberculosis as the most common and the deadliest disease in the world.

TB was also a mysterious illness. Some victims died months after getting sick. Others became weaker and weaker for years before dying. Sufferers became so thin that they looked like skeletons. Few people recovered.

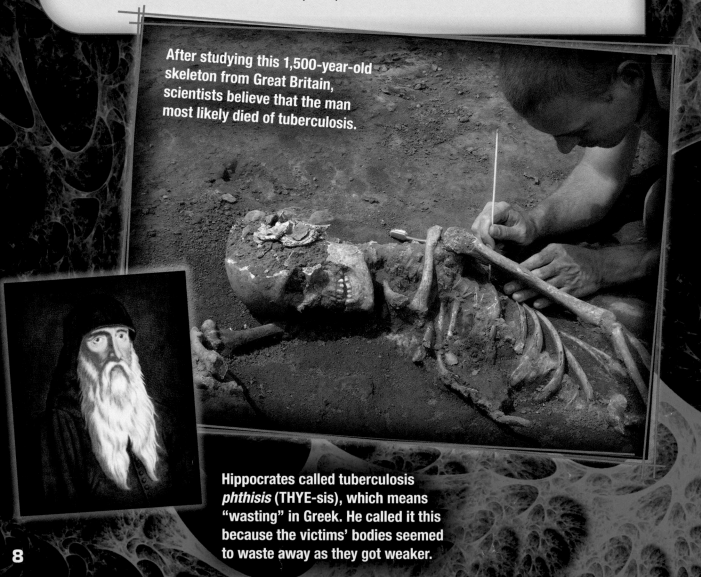

After studying this 1,500-year-old skeleton from Great Britain, scientists believe that the man most likely died of tuberculosis.

Hippocrates called tuberculosis *phthisis* (THYE-sis), which means "wasting" in Greek. He called it this because the victims' bodies seemed to waste away as they got weaker.

For many centuries, doctors did not know what caused this terrible **plague**. Still, they tried different ways of treating it. Some had patients eat wolf livers. Others had patients drink elephant blood or live underground. Unfortunately, nothing they tried worked.

People once believed that royalty could cure TB victims just by touching them.

Tuberculosis became known as the "white plague" because people with the disease often looked very pale. It was also called "consumption" because the disease seemed to consume, or eat through, its victims' bodies.

Crisis in the Cities

TB was always considered a very serious disease. However, it became a crisis in the 1700s when it rapidly began spreading throughout the world. During this time, cities in Europe and North America were growing quickly. In overpopulated areas, many people lived in tiny, cramped **tenements**. Some worked in poorly **ventilated** factories. Tuberculosis was common under these conditions. Why? Some doctors suspected that the disease was **contagious**. They thought people might be able to catch TB just by breathing in the air that a sick person breathed out. Still, at that time, no one was exactly sure how the disease spread.

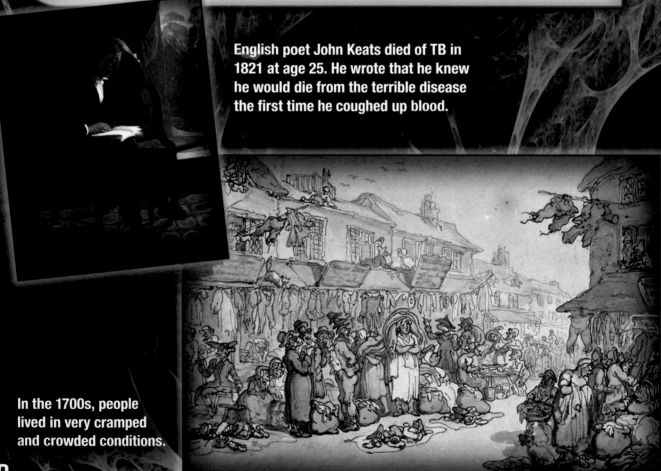

English poet John Keats died of TB in 1821 at age 25. He wrote that he knew he would die from the terrible disease the first time he coughed up blood.

In the 1700s, people lived in very cramped and crowded conditions.

Becoming sick from tuberculosis was often a death sentence. It killed about one billion people between 1700 and 1900. However, without knowing what caused TB, doctors couldn't figure out how to treat it.

Doctors thought that TB could spread easily through crowded cities such as New York City, shown here in the 1900s.

Stages of TB	
First stage	dry, constant cough, chest pains, and trouble breathing
Second stage	a more severe cough, high fever, rapid heartbeat, reddish face
Final stage	patient is extremely thin with hollow cheeks and sunken eyes; has a hoarse cough, which is also known as a "graveyard cough;" has sores in the throat that make it difficult to eat or talk; has stomach cramps, sweating, and vomiting of blood

In the 1830s, American doctor William Sweetser wrote about the different stages of symptoms that he observed in TB patients. He said the length of time for each stage was different for each patient. However, in the worst cases, victims died in as little as three weeks after the first symptoms appeared.

With no effective treatments, more than half of all people who came down with tuberculosis died. By 1850, about 25 percent of all Europeans and Americans were dying of TB!

An Amazing Discovery

By the 1880s, tuberculosis was causing seven million deaths around the world every year. Luckily, by this time, doctors were finally starting to learn more about the disease. In 1882, a German doctor named Robert Koch made an amazing discovery. Using a microscope, he discovered the tiny germs, or **bacteria**, that cause pulmonary tuberculosis.

Dr. Koch won the Nobel Prize in Medicine in 1905 to honor his discoveries about tuberculosis. This award is given to people who have made the most important discoveries in understanding and treating diseases.

Tuberculosis bacteria are so tiny that they can be seen only with powerful microscopes. Here is a close-up image of TB bacteria, shown in orange.

Koch's discovery helped people understand how the bacteria could be coughed up from the lungs. Whenever TB sufferers cough or sneeze, bacteria leave their mouths and noses and float into the air. People nearby can breathe in the bacteria and become infected. That is why TB spreads so easily in crowded places such as tenements.

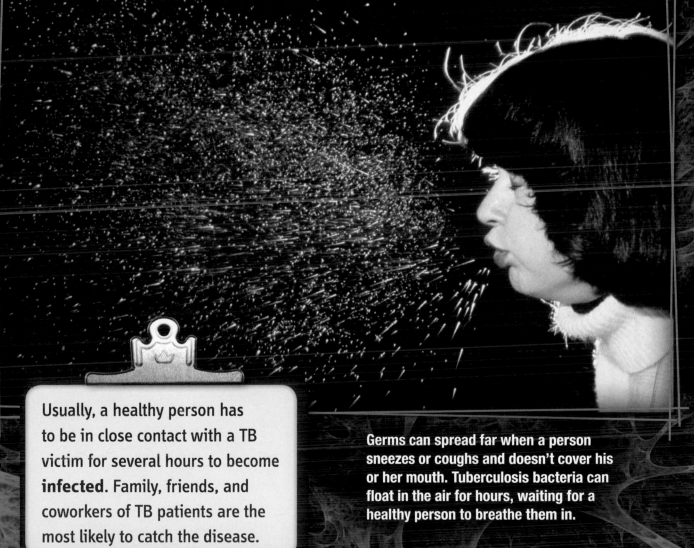

Usually, a healthy person has to be in close contact with a TB victim for several hours to become **infected**. Family, friends, and coworkers of TB patients are the most likely to catch the disease.

Germs can spread far when a person sneezes or coughs and doesn't cover his or her mouth. Tuberculosis bacteria can float in the air for hours, waiting for a healthy person to breathe them in.

Fresh Air and Sunshine

Koch's discoveries inspired an American doctor named Edward Livingston Trudeau to study tuberculosis. Trudeau himself was sick with TB. During his illness, he moved to the Adirondack Mountains in New York, hoping that the fresh air and sunshine would cure him. Though he still had TB bacteria in his body, his health soon improved dramatically. Could fresh air help other TB patients?

When Trudeau first became sick with TB, his doctors told him he would not live long. After moving to the Adirondack Mountains, though, he found that his health improved. Here, he is with his wife in the Adirondacks.

To find out, Trudeau infected ten rabbits with tuberculosis bacteria in 1885. He kept five of the rabbits in a dark, damp box with little food. He moved the other five to a small island. There, they had plenty of fresh air, sunshine, and food—just as Trudeau had in the Adirondacks. Three months later, four of the rabbits in the box were dead. Only one of the rabbits living outdoors had died of the disease.

Trudeau working in his lab

Tuberculosis is not just a human disease. It can infect animals such as rabbits, cattle, turtles, frogs, fish, guinea pigs, and even elephants. Sick animals can also spread TB to humans, though animals almost never catch TB from humans.

Life in a Sanatorium

After seeing the results from the test with the rabbits, Trudeau believed fresh air and plenty of food could help human TB patients, too. So he opened a **sanatorium** in the Adirondacks.

At the sanatorium, patients mainly rested and ate. They got three meals, several snacks, and lots of milk every day. They also had long periods of rest outdoors in the fresh air.

Dr. Trudeau built his sanatorium, Little Red, in the same area of the Adirondacks where he had recovered from tuberculosis.

Soon, other sanatoriums were opened across the country to treat patients. They helped some TB patients feel better. When patients' symptoms improved, they stopped spreading the disease to others. Treatment in the sanatoriums also helped people build up their own bodily defenses against the TB bacteria. However, many patients were not cured by their sanatorium stay and later died.

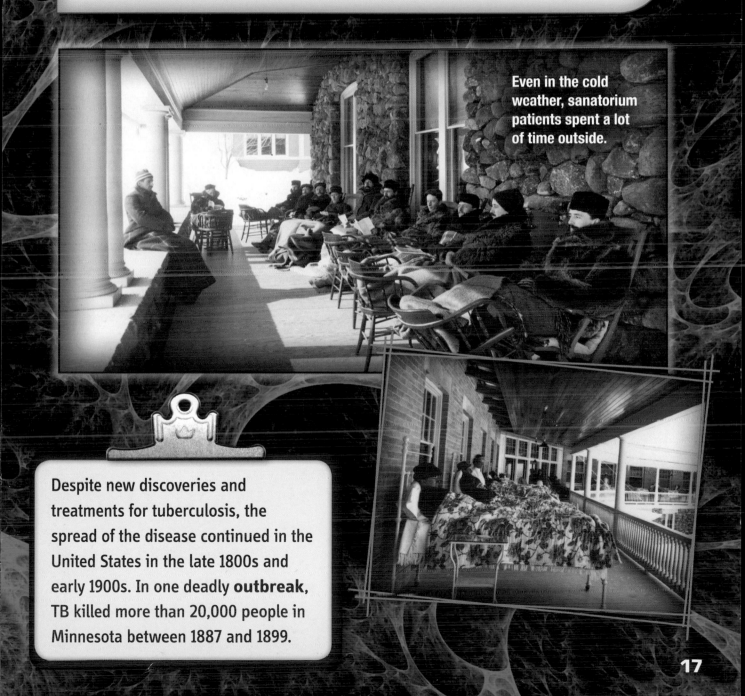

Even in the cold weather, sanatorium patients spent a lot of time outside.

Despite new discoveries and treatments for tuberculosis, the spread of the disease continued in the United States in the late 1800s and early 1900s. In one deadly **outbreak**, TB killed more than 20,000 people in Minnesota between 1887 and 1899.

New Medicines, New Hope

In the early 1940s, doctors began to use antibiotics, a new kind of medicine at the time, to treat many illnesses. On November 20, 1944, doctors in Minnesota tried giving an antibiotic to a seriously ill TB patient. Incredibly, the patient began to feel better in a few days, and was eventually cured. Unlike sanatorium treatments, the antibiotic was effective in killing tuberculosis bacteria. After treatment, no live TB germs were left in the patient's body.

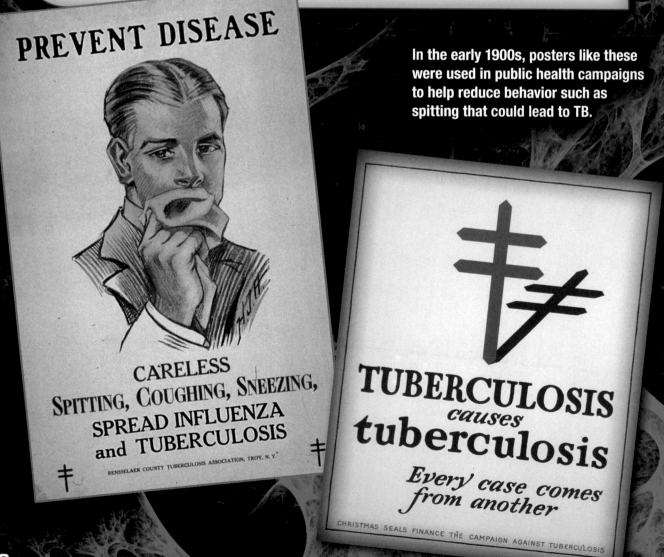

In the early 1900s, posters like these were used in public health campaigns to help reduce behavior such as spitting that could lead to TB.

PREVENT DISEASE

CARELESS
SPITTING, COUGHING, SNEEZING,
SPREAD INFLUENZA
and TUBERCULOSIS

RENSSELAER COUNTY TUBERCULOSIS ASSOCIATION, TROY, N.Y.

TUBERCULOSIS
causes
tuberculosis

Every case comes
from another

CHRISTMAS SEALS FINANCE THE CAMPAIGN AGAINST TUBERCULOSIS

As the doctors gave the same antibiotic to more TB patients, they discovered a problem. The tuberculosis bacteria changed quickly and became **resistant** to the medicine. This caused the drug to stop working. Doctors were able to solve this problem by using more than one kind of antibiotic on each patient. By the 1950s, tuberculosis was a treatable disease.

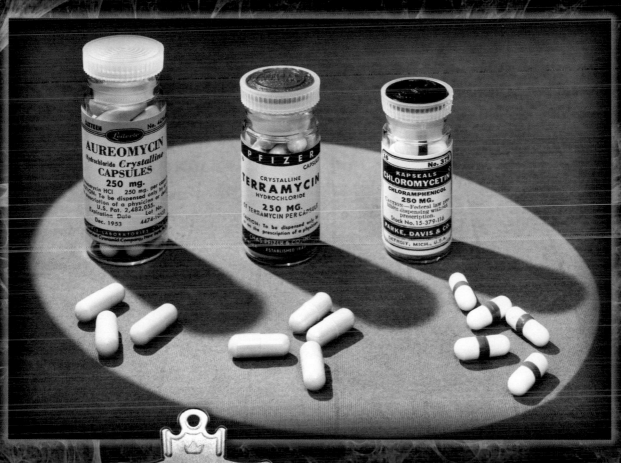

In 1900, about 194 out of every 100,000 Americans died of tuberculosis. By the 1960s, because of better medicines, TB killed only 6 Americans out of 100,000.

In the 1940s and 1950s, doctors began using antibiotics to treat diseases such as TB and typhoid fever.

A Global Emergency

Not everyone who becomes infected with tuberculosis becomes sick. Most infected people have **latent** tuberculosis, which means the TB bacteria enter their bodies and stay there. Yet these people do not look or feel sick. Fortunately, those with latent TB cannot spread it to others.

Only about 10 percent of people infected with tuberculosis ever become ill with **active** TB. However, some diseases such as **AIDS** or **diabetes**, or conditions such as **malnutrition** weaken people's **immune systems**. Their bodies may not be strong enough to keep the bacteria under control. Latent tuberculosis infections can then easily become active.

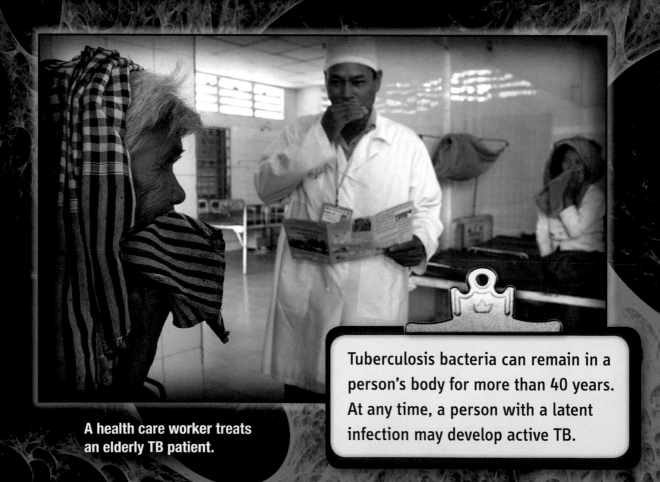

A health care worker treats an elderly TB patient.

Tuberculosis bacteria can remain in a person's body for more than 40 years. At any time, a person with a latent infection may develop active TB.

Despite the availability of effective treatment, not everyone has access to it. Tuberculosis continues to kill people all over the world. In 1993, the World Health Organization (WHO), a group of doctors, scientists, and health workers that monitors diseases worldwide, declared TB a global emergency. By 2008, it was killing about 1.8 million people every year. As a result, WHO has worked to send more medications to patients in need. The group also finds doctors from around the world who are willing to treat people with the disease. Then they send the doctors to places where TB is a problem.

TB Cases Around the World

Estimated TB Cases
(Per 100,000 People)

- more than 300
- 100–299
- 50–99
- 25–49
- 0–24
- No Estimate

This map shows cases of active TB around the world in 2006. About one-third of all people on Earth have latent tuberculosis infections. Many of these people live in Southeast Asia and southern Africa.

Even Worse News

Active tuberculosis patients treated with a few kinds of antibiotics can quickly begin to feel better. After several weeks, they are no longer contagious. However, full treatment takes at least six months. Missing even one dose of antibiotics can be very dangerous. If patients do not finish the treatment, the TB infection can come back as a stronger **strain**, called multidrug-resistant tuberculosis (MDR-TB). This powerful strain cannot be killed by the usual tuberculosis medicines. It must be treated with more expensive antibiotics—and treatment can take up to two years.

This patient has MDR-TB. Only one out of 20 patients in the world has this form of the disease.

Some tuberculosis patients who do not complete their drug treatments may get an even deadlier form of MDR-TB called **extensively** drug-resistant tuberculosis (XDR-TB). Very few medicines can kill this strain. Doctors cannot always treat it. In the first known outbreak of XDR-TB among **HIV** patients, 98 percent of the people died! Luckily, this is a very rare type of TB.

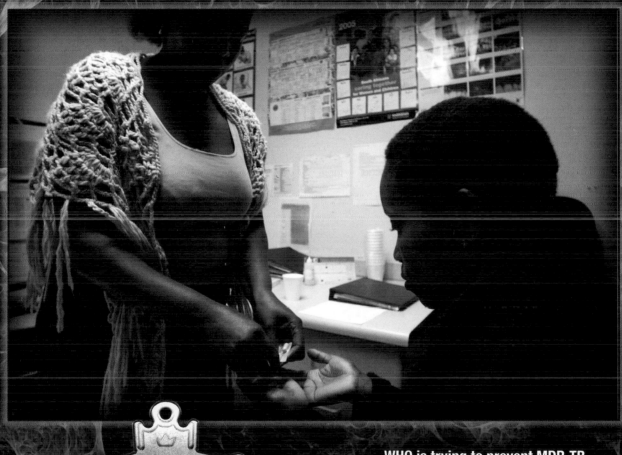

Like all TB patients, those who become ill with either MDR-TB or XDR-TB can spread it to others. In the 1990s, New York City spent about one billion dollars to control an outbreak of MDR-TB.

WHO is trying to prevent MDR-TB and XDR-TB from becoming bigger problems. To make sure TB patients complete their treatments, doctors or nurses are assigned to watch them each time they take their medicines.

Isolated!

For three months, none of the antibiotics that Oswaldo Juarez took worked. Through tests, doctors learned that he had a very rare strain of TB. Though it's not officially recognized by WHO, some doctors call it extremely drug-resistant tuberculosis (XXDR-TB).

In order to receive proper treatment and because others could catch deadly germs any time Oswaldo opened his mouth to laugh, sneeze, cough, or talk, he had to be **isolated**. Oswaldo said he "could kill a lot of people" if he left the hospital or had visitors.

Oswaldo's treatments took place at A.G. Holley State Hospital in Lantana, Florida.

There is no known effective treatment for XXDR-TB. Doctors tried many different kinds of drugs to cure Oswaldo, who took up to 30 pills every day. Doctors used needles to inject even more medicines into his blood. Amazingly, by July 2009, almost two years after being diagnosed with TB, Oswaldo was cured. His lung healed and he was no longer contagious.

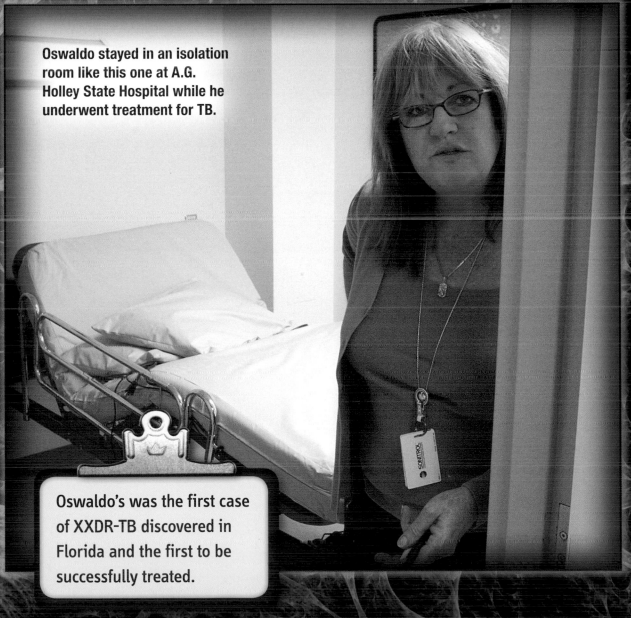

Oswaldo stayed in an isolation room like this one at A.G. Holley State Hospital while he underwent treatment for TB.

Oswaldo's was the first case of XXDR-TB discovered in Florida and the first to be successfully treated.

The Ones We Really Fear

While 95 percent of TB cases are treatable, doctors are still worried. Deadly, drug-resistant strains of TB are spreading. They have popped up in many countries, including South Africa and Russia. Dr. Ashkin says cases like Oswaldo's, "are the ones we really fear because I'm not sure how we treat them."

Here, Dr. Ashkin (front) works with a TB patient. Since tuberculosis is spread through the air, Dr. Ashkin believes that treating one TB patient is "protecting all of us."

Many organizations are helping to fight TB in poor countries, such as South Africa, where people are undernourished and can't afford to buy medicine. These groups, such as Partners in Health and Doctors Without Borders, raise money that is used to buy food and medicine for these people. Scientists are also working to create new medicines for TB. Much progress has been made in the treatment of the disease. However, there is still more to do to win the battle against the white plague.

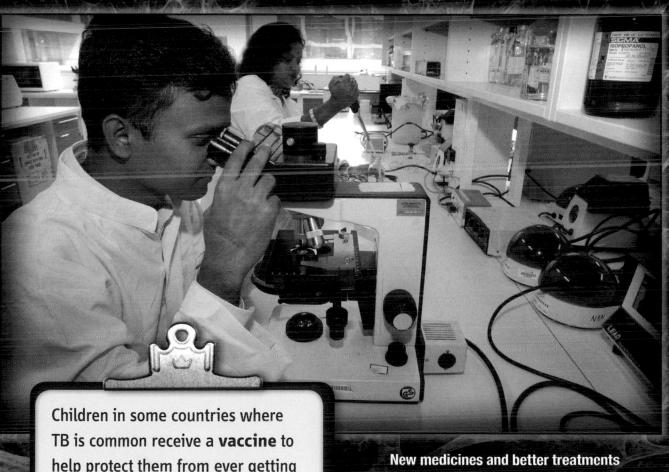

Children in some countries where TB is common receive a **vaccine** to help protect them from ever getting the disease. It does not always work, though. Scientists are working to create a more effective vaccine.

New medicines and better treatments are being created to help stop the spread of tuberculosis.

Famous Tuberculosis Outbreaks

Tuberculosis was once a great mystery. People did not know what caused it or how to treat it. Unfortunately, billions of people have died from the disease throughout history.

The Ancient World

- Scientists think that humans may have first caught a form of tuberculosis from cows about 10,000 years ago.

- Scientists have found Egyptian mummies with signs of tuberculosis. Some of these mummies are more than 4,000 years old.

- In about 400 B.C., the Greek doctor Hippocrates wrote that TB was the deadliest disease in the world.

- The Greeks had different theories at the time about what treatments would work best for tuberculosis. Some doctors thought patients should rest; others thought they should exercise. Some doctors gave their patients lots of food, while others recommended very little to eat.

1700–1882

- Tuberculosis spread rapidly throughout growing cities in Europe and the United States. It was the leading cause of death in these parts of the world at the time.

- About one billion people died of the disease during this time period.

- In 1720, English doctor Benjamin Marten guessed that TB could be spread from person to person. He had no proof, but he thought "wonderfully minute living creatures" could pass from a sick person to a healthy person during periods of close contact.

- Dr. Marten's guess was proved correct when Dr. Robert Koch, using a microscope, discovered TB bacteria more than 150 years later.

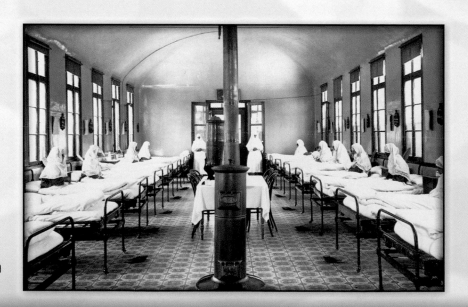

A TB hospital in the 1800s

Tuberculosis Facts

Fifty years ago, tuberculosis was on the decline, but the disease has made a comeback. Today, someone in the world is infected with the illness every second. Here are some more facts about TB.

Tuberculosis Today

- About two million people die from TB every year.

- One way to determine if a person has latent TB is with a skin test. A doctor will inject a liquid that contains TB bacteria into a person's arm. If a person has a TB infection, a bump will appear on his or her arm in two or three days.

- To diagnose active TB, a doctor can take a sample of **phlegm** from a person's lung, smear it onto a glass slide, and add dye to it. Then the doctor looks at it under a microscope to see if TB bacteria are present.

- Simple tuberculosis can be treated cheaply and easily with antibiotics. Dangerous drug-resistant strains are harder to treat—and more expensive. It can cost hundreds of thousands of dollars to treat just one person with drug-resistant tuberculosis.

- MDR-TB and XDR-TB are common in Eastern Europe and parts of Latin America, Asia, and Africa.

- In 1995, WHO started Directly Observed Therapy (DOT) programs in which patients take their medicines at clinics or from doctors or nurses so someone can watch them take their pills. This encourages them to never miss a dose.

- Tuberculosis remains rare in the United States. **Immigrants** and travelers from countries where TB is common can bring the disease with them when they enter the country.

Preventing Tuberculosis

- People who may have spent time around a person sick with TB should get a skin test.

- People with latent TB should seek antibiotic treatment right away.

- People undergoing treatment for TB should take every dose of their medicine. Otherwise, the disease can become resistant to drugs.

- To prevent spreading the disease, a patient who is sick should cover his or her mouth and nose when coughing or sneezing.

Italian artist Amedeo Modigliani painted this self-portrait before he died of TB in 1920 at the age of 35.

Glossary

active (AK-tiv) something that progresses

AIDS (AYDZ) an often deadly disease in which the body's ability to protect itself against illness is destroyed

antibiotics (an-ti-bye-OT-iks) medicines that destroy or stop the growth of bacteria that cause diseases

bacteria (bak-TIHR-ee-uh) tiny life forms that can be seen only under a microscope; some can cause disease

blood vessels (BLUHD VESS-uhlz) tiny tubes, such as veins, that carry blood around a person's or an animal's body

contagious (kuhn-TAY-juhss) able to be passed from one person to another

diabetes (dye-uh-BEE-teez) a disease in which a person has too much sugar in his or her blood

extensively (ek-STEN-siv-lee) very

HIV (aych-eye-VEE) stands for Human Immunodeficiency Virus; the virus that causes AIDS

immigrants (IM-uh-gruhnts) people who come from one country to live permanently in a new one

immune systems (i-MYOON SISS-tuhmz) the systems that people's bodies use to protect themselves from harmful germs that can cause diseases

infected (in-FEKT-id) spread a germ or disease to others

isolated (EYE-sul-late-id) kept separate and away from others

latent (LATE-uhnt) invisible or not active, but still present

malnutrition (mal-noo-TRISH-uhn) a harmful condition caused by not having enough food or eating the wrong kinds of food

outbreak (OUT-brake) a sudden start or increase in the activity of something, such as the spread of a disease

phlegm (FLEM) the thick substance that can be found in the lungs and is often coughed up during a cold

plague (PLAYG) a disease that spreads quickly and often kills many people

pulmonary tuberculosis (PUHL-muh-nair-ee tu-bur-kyuh-LOH-sis) a contagious disease, caused by bacteria, that attacks the lungs and causes patients to lose weight, have fevers, and have trouble breathing

resistant (ri-ZIS-tuhnt) not affected

sanatorium (san-uh-TOHR-ee-uhm) a building where patients suffering from certain long-term diseases stay to increase their health and ease symptoms

strain (STRAYN) a type or variety of something, such as a disease

tenements (TEN-uh-muhnts) small, run-down, often crowded apartment buildings

tissue (TISH-oo) a group of connected cells of the same type inside a plant or animal that work together as one

vaccine (vak-SEEN) medicine that helps protect a person or animal from getting a particular disease

ventilated (VEN-tuh-layt-id) exposed to fresh air

X-rays (EKS-rayz) images of the inside of a person's body

Bibliography

Altman, Lawrence K., M.D. "Rise of a Deadly TB Reveals a Global System in Crisis." *The New York Times* (March 20, 2007).

Maso, Margie, and Martha Mendoza. "Drugs Can't Always Stop TB Anymore." *San Francisco Chronicle* (January 10, 2010).

Steward D.A., L.D. Ross, and E.L. Ross. *Tuberculosis: An Insidious Disease.* The Canadian Medical Journal Association (August 1934), 160–164.

Yancey, Diane. *Tuberculosis.* Minneapolis, MN: Twenty-First Century Books (2007).

www.cdc.gov/tb/topic/drtb/default.htm

Read More

Finer, Kim Renee. *Tuberculosis.* New York: Facts on File (2003).

O'Shei, Tim. *The World's Deadliest Diseases.* Mankato, MN: Capstone Press (2006).

Silverstein, Alvin, Virginia B. Silverstein, and Laura Silverstein Nunn. *The Tuberculosis Update.* Berkeley Heights, NJ: Enslow Publishers (2006).

Wouk, Henry. *Tuberculosis.* Tarrytown, NY: Benchmark Books (2009).

Learn More Online

To learn more about TB, visit
www.bearportpublishing.com/NightmarePlagues

Index

About the Author

Miriam Aronin is a writer and editor. She also enjoys reading, dancing, and staying healthy.